Spirituals for Solo Singers

11 Spirituals Arranged for Solo Voice and Piano...
For Recitals, Concerts and Contests

COMPILED AND EDITED BY JAY ALTHOUSE

Contents

Cover art: *Holy Mountain III*, 1945
by Horace Pippin (American 1888-1946)
Oil on canvas (25 ½" X 30 ¼")
Photo: Lee Stalsworth
Hirshhorn Museum and Sculpture Garden,
Smithsonian Institution
Gift of Joseph H. Hirshhorn, 1966

ABOUT THE COVER

Horace Pippin (1888-1946) was one of the great self-taught African-American artists of the 20th century. Except for a brief stint in the Army during World War I, he lived his entire life in West Chester, Pennsylvania. Despite a serious wartime injury to his right hand, Pippin began painting in the late 1920s and by 1938 his works were being exhibited in galleries in New York and Philadelphia. His *Holy Mountain III* is one of a series of *Holy Mountain* paintings which may have been inspired by the *Peaceable Kingdom* paintings of earlier American folk artists such as Edward Hicks.

Alfred

Cover design: Martha Widmann

EZEKIEL'S WHEEL

Arranged by
PHILIP KERN

lit-tle wheel run by faith and the big wheel run by the grace of God. A

wheel in a wheel, way in the mid-dle of the air.

1. Some go to church to sing and shout, way in the mid-dle of the air; be-
2. you want to sing that ho-ly song, way in the mid-dle of the air; you'll

fore six months they're all turned out, way in the mid-dle of the air. If
have to sing your whole life long,

way in the mid-dle of the air._____ E-

ze-kiel saw the wheel way up in the mid-dle of the air. E-

ze-kiel saw the wheel way in the mid-dle of the air. And the

lit-tle wheel run by faith and the big wheel run by the grace of God. A

26 wheel in a wheel, way in the mid - dle of the

28 air. _____ There's a lit - tle wheel _ a - turn - in' in my

mf

30

mf simile

31 heart, _____ there's a lit - tle wheel ___ a - turn - in' in my

33 heart. _____ In my heart, _____ in my

lit-tle song _ a sing-in' in my soul. _____

Some go to church to sing and shout, way in the mid-dle of the air; be-

fore six months they're all turned out, way in the mid-dle of the air. If

you want to sing that ho-ly song, way in the mid-dle of the air; you'll

lit - tle wheel run by faith and the big wheel run by the grace of God. A

wheel in a wheel way in the mid - dle of the

air, way up there! _____ E - ze-kiel saw the wheel

way up in the mid- dle of the air! _____

KUM BA YAH

Arranged by
PATSY FORD SIMMS (ASCAP)

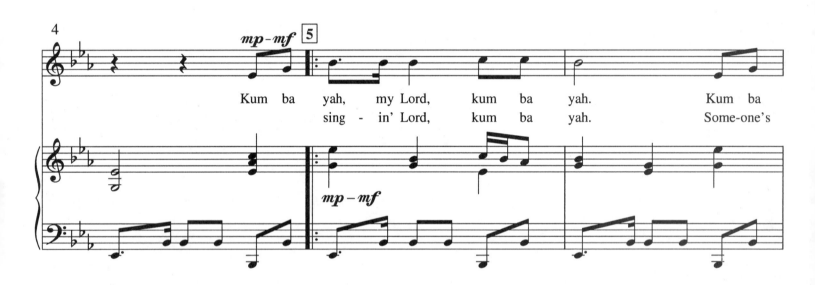

Kum ba yah, my Lord, kum ba yah. Kum ba
sing - in' Lord, kum ba yah. Some-one's

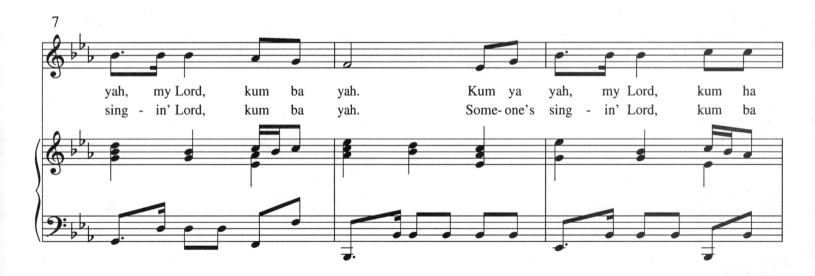

yah, my Lord, kum ba yah. Kum ya yah, my Lord, kum ha
sing - in' Lord, kum ba yah. Some-one's sing - in' Lord, kum ba

cry - in' Lord, kum ba yah. Oh, Lord, _____ kum ba

yah. Kum ba yah, _____ kum ba yah, kum ba

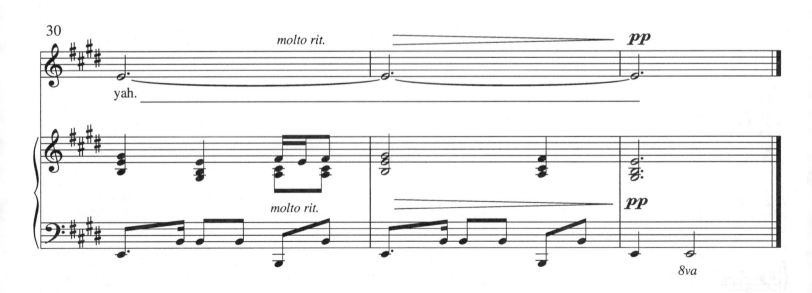

yah. _____

8va

MY LORD, WHAT A MORNING

Arranged by
JAY ALTHOUSE

Look-ing to my God's right hand when the stars be-gin to fall.

My Lord, what a morn-ing. My Lord, what a morn-ing. O, my Lord, what a morn-ing ___ when the stars be - gin to fall. _____

WADE IN THE WATER

Arranged by
MARK HAYES

Wade ___ in the wa - ter, ___ God's gon - na trou - ble ___

God's ___ gon - na trou - ble, ___

God's gon - na trou - ble the wa - ter! ___

AMAZING GRACE

Words by
JOHN NEWTON

Early American Melody
Arranged by JAY ALTHOUSE

once _____ was ___ lost but now _____ am ___ found, was

blind, but ____ now I see. _____

Through man - y _____ dan - gers

toils and snares, I have al - read - y

CLIMBIN' UP THE MOUNTAIN

Arranged by
PATSY FORD SIMMS (ASCAP)

LITTLE DAVID, PLAY ON YOUR HARP

Arranged by
PHILIP KERN

With spirit (♩ = ca. 108)

36

LET US BREAK BREAD TOGETHER

Arranged by
JAY ALTHOUSE

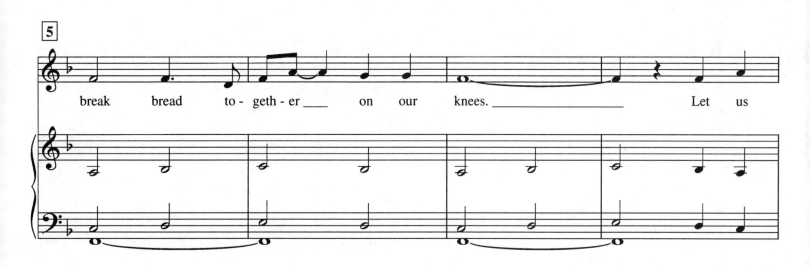

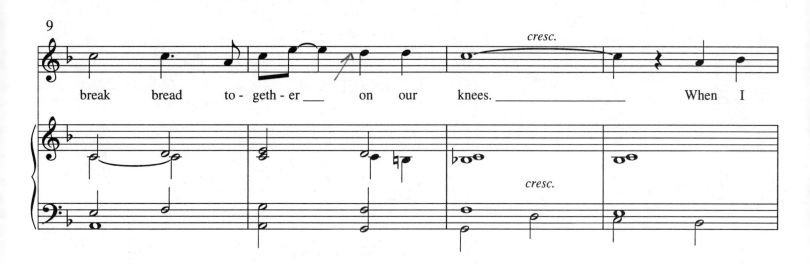

GO, TELL IT ON THE MOUNTAIN

Arranged by
PATSY FORD SIMMS (ASCAP)

NOBODY KNOWS THE TROUBLE I'VE SEEN

Arranged by
JAY ALTHOUSE

52

No - bod - y knows the trou - ble I've seen. Glo - ry hal - le -

lu - jah! ___ If

you get there be - fore I do, ___ Oh yes,

Lord. Tell all my friends I'm com - in', too. ___

Oh yes, Lord. No - bod - y knows the

trou - ble I've seen. No - bod - y knows but Je - sus.
(my sor - row.)

NOBODY KNOWS THE TROUBLE I'VE SEEN

Alto Saxophone

Rhythmically (♩ = ca. 72)

Arranged by
JAY ALTHOUSE

RISE UP, SHEPHERD, AND FOLLOW!

Arranged by
MARK HAYES

Rise up, shep - herd, and fol - low! __ Leave your ewes and

leave your rams; Rise up, shep - herd, and fol - low! __

Fol - low. Fol - low! Rise up, shep - herd, and

fol - low! __ Fol - low the star of Beth - le - hem; _____

fol - low __ Leave your sheep and leave your lambs;

Rise up, shep - herd, and fol - low! __ Leave your ewes and

leave your rams: Rise up, shep - herd, and fol - low! __

Fol - low, fol - low! Rise up, shep - herd, and

58
fol - low! _____ Fol - low the star of Beth - le - hem;

61
Rise up, shep - herd, and fol - low! ____

63
Fol - low, fol - low! Rise up, shep - herd, and

66
fol - low! __ Fol - low the star of Beth - le - hem; _____

Rise up, shep - herd, rise up, shep - herd,

rise up, shep - herd. _____ and fol - low! _____

Fol - low! ___ *8va* _____

Many of the vocal solos in *Spirituals for Solo Singers* are also available in choral editions from Alfred Publishing Co., Inc.

Amazing Grace, arranged by Jay Althouse

Climbin' Up the Mountain, arranged by Patsy Ford Simms

Ezekiel's Wheel, arranged by Philip Kern

Go, Tell It on the Mountain, arranged by Patsy Ford Simms

Kum Ba Yah, arranged by Patsy Ford Simms

Let Us Break Bread Together (from Two Communion Hymn Meditations), arranged by Jay Althouse

Little David, Play on Your Harp, arranged by Philip Kern

My Lord, What a Morning, arranged by Jay Althouse

Rise Up, Shepherd, and Follow, arranged by Mark Hayes

Wade in the Water, arranged by Mark Hayes

Order these Alfred choral editions from your favorite music dealer.

MORE VOCAL SOLO COLLECTIONS FROM ALFRED PUBLISHING CO.

The Christmas Soloist - Edited by Jay Althouse
Nine Unique Settings of Christmas Favorites Arranged in Art Song Style for Concerts and Recitals

MEDIUM HIGH (3385)   MEDIUM LOW (3386)

Folk Songs for Solo Singers - Edited by Jay Althouse
11 Timeless and Popular Folk Songs for Solo Voice and Piano for Recitals, Concerts and Contests

MEDIUM HIGH   MEDIUM LOW
Book (4952)   Book (4953)
Accompaniment Cassette (11960)   Accompaniment Cassette (11962)
Book/Cassette (4960)   Book/Cassette (4962)